CONTENTS

TAKE IT EASY

Words and Music by
JACKSON BROWNE and GLENN FREY

4

PEACEFUL EASY FEELING

Words and Music by
JACK TEMPCHIN

11

DESPERADO

Words and Music by
DON HENLEY and GLENN FREY

THE LONG RUN

Words and Music by
DON HENLEY and GLENN FREY

I used to hur-ry a lot; I used to wor-ry a lot. I used to
don't un-der-stand why you don't treat your-self bet - ter, do___

stay out till the break of __ day. __

'Cause all the

__ the cra - zy things that you do. __

Oh, ____ that did-n't git it; it was

deb -u - tantes __ in

high time I quit it.

I just could - n't car - ry on that __ way. __

Hous - ton, ba - by,

could - n't hold a can - dle to you. __

Oh, ____ I did some dam-age, I know it's true. _____

Did-n't

Did you do it for love? __ Did you do it for mon-ey? __

Did you

know I was so lone - ly till I found you. _____

do it for spite? Did you think you had to, hon - ey?

ONE OF THESE NIGHTS

Words and Music by
DON HENLEY and GLENN FREY

23

WITCHY WOMAN

Words and Music by
BERNIE LEADON and DON HENLEY

LYIN' EYES

Words and Music by
DON HENLEY and GLENN FREY

NEW KID IN TOWN

Words and Music by
DON HENLEY, GLENN FREY
and JOHN DAVID SOUTHER

Moderately

There's talk on the street;_ it sounds so fa-mil - iar.
You look in her eyes;_ the mu - sic be-gins to play.

her, and you're still a - round. _____ Oh, my, ___ my. ___

There's a new kid in town, _____

just an-oth-er new kid in town. _____

Ooh, ___ hoo. Ev-'ry-bod-y's talk-ing 'bout the new kid in town.

42

HEARTACHE TONIGHT

Words and Music by
DON HENLEY, GLENN FREY,
BOB SEGER and J.D. SOUTHER

44

48

know. _____ There'll be a heart - ache to-night, _____ a heart - ache to-night, I know. _____

TAKE IT TO THE LIMIT

Words and Music by
RANDY MEISNER, DON HENLEY
and GLENN FREY

THE BEST OF MY LOVE

Words and Music by
DON HENLEY, GLENN FREY and JOHN DAVID SOUTHER

HOTEL CALIFORNIA

Words and Music by
DON HENLEY, GLENN FREY
and DON FELDER